Getting Ready
Things to do NOW

Make It Easy for Employers to Contact You

Make sure the voicemail is set up on your phone. (Whichever number you will put on your resume and applications.)

Make sure the voicemail has a name, not just a phone number.

Do you have an email address? If not, you need one. Gmail is a good place to get an email address. If you aren't sure how to get an email address, ask someone at you trust to help you set up an account.

It is best to use your name as your email address. You may have to try different ways to use your name.

Example: Sally Smith

These are some examples of email addresses she could use:

sallysmith@gmail.com
ssmith@gmail.com
smithsally@gmail.com
smithsal@gmail.com
salsmith@gmail.com
sallys@gmail.com
ssally@gmail.com

Check Your Social Media

If you use social media such as Facebook, take a look at your page. Is there anything you would not want your grandmother to see? Are there any curse words? Are there any pictures that don't look mature? Use the "Grandma Test." If you wouldn't want Grandma to see it, don't put it on social media.

Your page should also be set to "private." If you need help, ask someone you trust or someone at Vocational Rehabilitation.

Get your Interview Clothes Ready

Women:
- Blue, brown, black, gray, or beige pants, skirt with a simple shirt OR a simple dress in one of those colors (dresses and skirts at least to your knees)
- Don't carry a big purse
- No nail polish, big jewelry, or perfume
- Not too much makeup

Men:
- Blue, brown, black, gray, or beige pants (kakis) with button-up shirt with a tie or a shirt with a collar
- No cologne, nail polish, or jewelry
- Shave or trim your mustache or beard so it looks neat

Everyone:
- Shower, brush your teeth, and use deodorant the morning of the interview
- Check your fingernails and shoes, are they neat and clean?
- If you smoke, check your clothes for smoke smells
- If you have tattoos, try to wear clothes that cover them
- Have neat hair in a natural color (no blue, pink, purple, bright red)
- Get a haircut, if you need one
- No shorts! Pants should be full-length.
- No sandals or flip-flops. Your toes should be covered.
- NO CELL PHONES! Leave it in the car.

Resumes

What is a resume?

A resume is a paper that tells an employer about you. It is usually printed on nice paper because it is important. It is telling people about you!

When you go to an interview, you should take a copy of your resume. Keep it neat and clean. Remember it is an important paper.

A resume will always have your name, address, and phone number. If you have an email address, it will have that, too.

A resume can also have things like:

- Work you have done in the past (even if you didn't get paid)
- Volunteer Work you have done
- Your Skills
- Where you went to school
- Accomplishments from school
- Clubs you were in
- Good things about your personality and how you act at work
- Other things that would make you great for the job

10 Steps to Interview Success

1) When you get the call for the interview, WRITE IT DOWN.

What is the day and time of the interview? <u>Write it down and repeat it back to them</u> to be sure you are right.

Ask where you should go. <u>Write it down and repeat it back to them.</u>
- **What is the address?**
- **Where should you go when you get there?**
- **Who do you ask for?**

Ask if you need to bring anything
- **If so, <u>write it down and repeat it back to them</u>**
- **Always plan to bring your Social Security Card, ID or Driver's License, and Resume to interviews.**

2) Find out about the company

Look at their website or talk to people who know about the company

Try to find out:
- What they do
- How they got started
- What is important to them (Do they help others? Do they make a product very well? Do they sell something?)

3) Get there 15 minutes before your interview time

4) It is important that you go in alone.

If someone brings you, they should wait in the car. No moms. No grandmas. No kids. No one should come in with you.

When you go inside, smile and introduce yourself and tell the person you are there for an interview

Wait patiently. If they are running late, it is ok. Be patient.

5) When you meet the interviewer:

- make eye contact
- smile
- shake their hand
- introduce yourself
- tell them it is nice to meet them

TIP: It can be helpful to practice introducing yourself. Friends and family may be willing to practice with you.

If the interviewer doesn't tell you where to sit, ask them where you should sit.

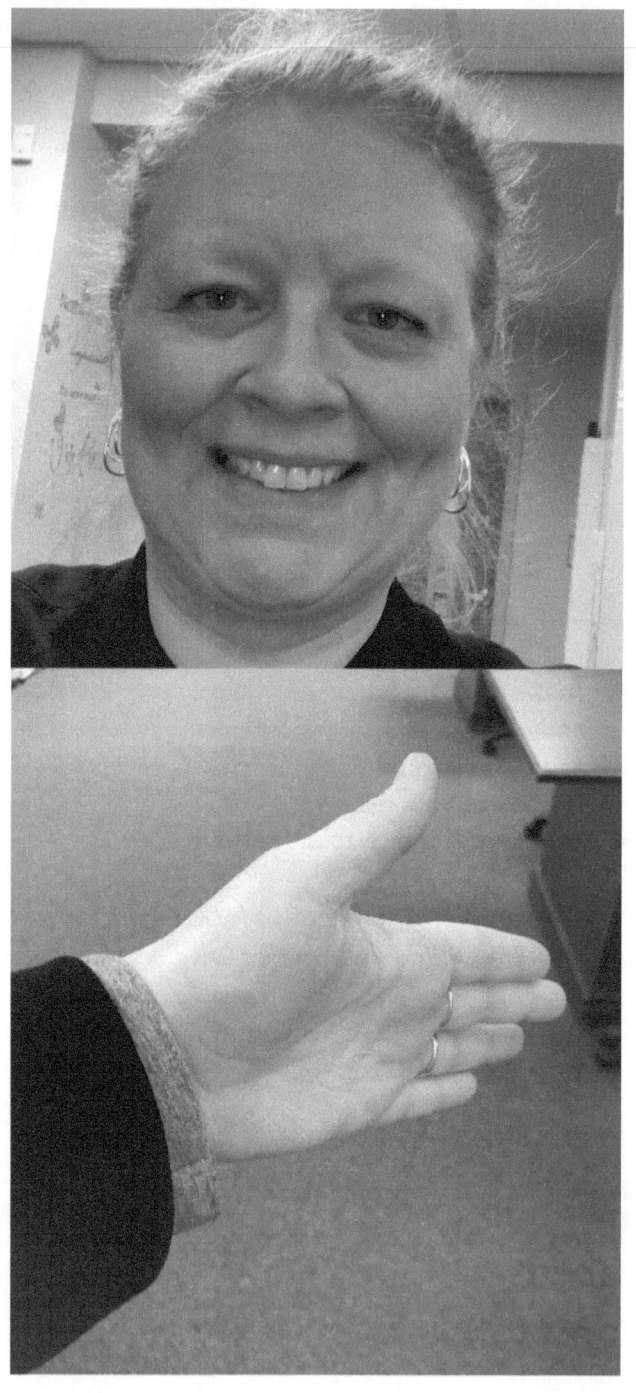

6) Sit up straight. Try not to twist in your chair.

7) Stay positive. No matter what they ask, don't say anything bad about places you have worked or people you have worked with. Find something nice to say.

8) Answer the questions

To Answer "Tell me about yourself"
Tell them about why you would be good at the job.
- Do you have experience doing that job or something like it?
- Have you taken a class or studied about the job?
- Do you have certain skills they need? (Good at helping others, good at putting things together, good at cleaning, good at following directions, or something else?)
- DO NOT: Talk about your disability, **focus on what you** CAN DO WELL.

To Answer "What is your biggest strength?"
- What is something you are really good at that would help you be great at that job?

To Answer "What is your biggest weakness?"
- What is something that used to be hard for you but you are good at now because you practiced and worked hard to get better? Tell them about that and how you got better.

To Answer "Why do you want to work here?"
- What do you like about the company? (You like doing what they do, you like shopping there, you like eating there, you like cleaning, you like cooking, you like working with animals, you like sorting things)

9) Ask THEM questions

At the end of the interview, they will usually ask if you have any questions. You always want to ask questions, so have some ready. You can write these down ahead of time and bring them with you.

Good questions to ask are:
- What kind of training will I get?
- What is the most important thing I should remember when I'm working here?
- What do you like about working here?
- Do you have a business card?

TIP: A business card is a small card that tells a person's name, their job, and how to contact them. It will help you remember who you spoke with and how to contact them to follow up.

ALWAYS ask:
When will you make a decision about the job?
OR
What should I expect next?

NEVER ask:
- How much will I get paid?
- Will I get benefits like insurance and vacation?
- When can I take a vacation?
- How many times can I be late before I get in trouble?

10) Follow up!

Take them a Thank You note later on the day of your interview or the next day. Be sure you look nice whenever you drop it off. (Dress like you would for an interview.)

Writing a Thank You note is easy. Get a nice piece of paper with a matching envelope or a small blank card with an envelope. (You can buy these at dollar stores.)

Put the interviewer's name on the front of the envelope.

Write something inside like:

Thank you for taking the time to interview me. I know I can do a good job for you and hope I get a chance to prove it to you.

Sincerely,
Your Name

You Got the Job!
Now what?
11 Steps to Success at Work

1) Be neat and clean every day.

- Keep yourself clean. Shower every day. Brush your teeth every day. Keep your hair neat and clean.
- Use deodorant every day.
- Make sure your clothes are clean.
- Men, remember to shave every day or keep your mustache or beard neat. (Remember some workplaces won't allow a mustache or beard.)

2) Know the dress code. It is important to dress appropriately for work every day.

- Do you wear a uniform to work? If so, what should you wear?
- If you have a uniform, be sure to wear it correctly every day. Don't forget anything at home and don't try to change the uniform. Follow the rules.
- Is there anything you can't wear to work? For example, some places don't allow you to wear jewelry or nail polish because you will be working around food.
- If you don't have a uniform, what are you allowed to wear and not allowed to wear to work? Stick to the rules.

3) Be on time.

- Be on time for work every day.
- That means getting there early enough to put your things away and being ready to work at your start time. If you start work at 9:00 am, you will probably want to get to work by 8:45 am.

4) Learn how to clock in.

If you don't clock in, you don't get paid. Make notes and use them for as long as you need them.

5) Be flexible.

Some days, you may be asked to do things you usually don't. For example, you may usually bag groceries. But some days, you may be asked to do something extra, like sweep the floors or clean up a mess in one of the aisles. Don't complain or say "That isn't my job." Do it with a smile.
If your boss asks you to stay a few minutes late, do it if you can.

6) Smile and Be Friendly

Remember, that people like people who smile. Smiling shows you are happy to be at work. And it makes it easier to make friends at work.

7) Stay focused on your work.

It is easy to get distracted sometimes. Make it a point to stay focused on your work.
Don't goof off at work.

8) Say "NO" to your cell phone.

Leave your cell phone at home or in a locker while you are working. Using your cell phone at work can cause you to lose your job. You can answer your texts at break time.

9) Follow the rules.

- Every workplace has rules. Know the rules and follow them. You can usually find the rules in your Employee Handbook. Your supervisor will probably go over the most important ones with you.
- Not following the rules can cause you to get hurt or fired.

10) Say "NO" to romance.

Dating people at work is not a good idea. It takes your focus away from your work. And if you break up, it can be very hard to keep working with that person every day.

11) Know who to stay away from.

- Most people at work will be nice. But sometimes someone won't be. They may ask you to break rules or do something you know you shouldn't. They may ask you for money.
- Stay away from these people and let someone you trust know what is happening.
- Never let anyone talk you into doing something you don't want to do.

Payday

Work can be fun. Meeting new people is great. But getting your first paycheck can be the best of all.

Payday isn't all fun and games, though. It takes planning to make payday go well.

Most employers won't pay you cash.

Some employers will give you a paper check. You will need to get this cashed. Some places charge you to cash a check.

Other employers will say you have to get your money deposited into a bank account instead of getting a check.

Sometimes, an employer will give you the choice of a paper check or having your money directly deposited.

If you get a paper check or direct deposit, starting a job means it is time to start thinking about getting a bank account if you don't have one.

First, you may want to get a recommendation about a bank or credit union from someone you trust.

The two most common types of bank accounts are checking accounts and savings accounts. You can put your money into either a checking account or a savings account. You can even put some in each one.

To open an account, you will usually need your Social Security Card and ID or Driver's License. You will also need money to open the account.

Before you go to the bank, call them to ask what to bring with you and how much money you will need to open an account. Also, ask if there is a monthly charge to have an account and if there are any other fees.

A checking account is for the money you plan to spend soon. Checking accounts usually come with debit cards. Some also include a few paper checks you can write.

You can use a debit card to pay for things at the store or to get cash out of an ATM (Automatic Teller Machine.) When you use your debit card, you will be asked to enter your PIN number. This is usually 4 numbers long.

If you get a debit card, there are a few very important rules to remember:
- Keep your debit card in a safe place
- Don't write your PIN number on your debit card or carry it with your debit card
- Never give your debit card to anyone else to use
- Don't choose a PIN number that is too easy, such as the year you were born or something like 1234 or 0000.
- Never give your PIN number to anyone else

Budgeting

What you do with your paycheck is very important. It is important to have a plan for your money.

This plan is called a budget.

1) **Write down your expenses. Expenses are what you spend your money on.**

Examples of expenses:
- Rent
- Utilities
- Bus Pass
- Food
- Meals at Restaurants
- Entertainment/Fun
- Clothes
- Savings (it is important to save some of your money)

2) **Write down your money goals. What are the things you want to save money for? Do you want to take a special trip? Do you want to buy something expensive? Some goals may be small. Others may be big.**

Examples of small goals:
- $100 Admission to Amusement Park
- $50 Admission to Fair and Food
- $30 Pair of new boots
- $60 New video game

Examples of big goals:
- $2,000 Scooter
- $350   Cruise with family

To reach these goals, it is important to save some money each month. This is where having a savings account can help. Putting your money in a savings account keeps you from accidentally spending it.

3) Write down all of your income. Income is the money you make or get from a check.

Examples of income:
- The money you make at work
- Checks you receive such as SSI

Subtract your expenses from your income. If your expenses are more than your income, you are spending too much.

Examples:

Income: $800.00   Income: $800.00
-    Expenses $725.00   -   Expenses $850

_____   _____

$75.00   Spending too much!

If you are spending too much, look at your budget to see what you don't need or what you could spend less on.

Example:
          $20 for Movie and Popcorn

Instead:
          $5 for Movie Rental and Making Popcorn at Home

Save $15!

Example:

     $60 for Eating in Restaurants 8 times per month (2 times per week)

Instead:

     $30 for Eating in Restaurants 4 times per month (1 time per week)

Save $30!

Make smart money decisions!